The Right Answer™ To...

"Do I Look Fat in This?"*

And Other Impossible Questions Women Ask!

By Pamela L. Garza

*Hint: Both "yes" and "no" are the wrong answer.

www.therightanswerbooks.com

Lost and Profound, LLC
P.O. Box 131
Kosse, TX 76653-0131

ISBN: 978-0615536156

This publication is designed to provide information with regard to the subject matter covered. It is sold with the understanding that the publisher, author, and editor are not engaged in rendering professional advice of any kind. If professional advice or other expert assistance is required, the services of a competent professional person should be sought.

www.therightanswerbooks.com

This book is dedicated to the men in my life who have always given me the right answers.

Especially...
my father, Jerry
my husband, Bert
and my son, Keegan

Table of Contents

Chapter 1

<u>Here's the Deal with Those Stupid Questions</u>

A man who's new to town is sitting on a park bench. A woman comes over and sits next to him.

"New around here?" she asks.

"Yes," he answers.

"Where you from?" she asks.

"Washington," he answers.

"The state or the city?" she asks.

"State," he answers.

"What did you do there?" she asks.

"I was in prison," he answers.

"Oh my gosh!" she says, "Whatever for?"

"My wife asked so many endless, pointless questions that I killed her, cut her up into little pieces, and fed her to the dog," he tells her.

"So..." she asks, "...you're single?"

Every guy who's ever dated, loved, lived with, or even looked at a woman is familiar with the crazy, whack-a-mole game women play with never-ending questions. You know the kind of questions I mean; the ones that, as soon as you hear them, you have an immediate gut reaction and think, "Oh no! I hate this ride!" Those are what I call impossible questions. But women can't help themselves. Really! It's like a tic or something.

Once I heard a man say to his wife, "Yeah, if you're so smart, why don't I understand you?" When I finally quit laughing, I realized that there's actually a lot of wisdom in that question. To be understood, we have to communicate in a way so that the other person can comprehend our meaning. Unfortunately, men and women are wired to communicate in very different ways. Sometimes women's impossible questions are actually statements; statements that guys just don't understand.

This book is a straight-forward translation of what women are *really* saying with all those impossible questions and what they're really looking for when they ask them. Believe it or not, when a woman asks a guy these kinds of questions, she's not seeking information or even an answer. She does NOT need logic. This is pretty confusing to most guys.

If you really want to know why you keep finding yourself staring blank-faced at the back of a recently slammed door, let's get right to it by taking a look at our title question.

She asks, "Do I look fat in this?" Some guys might think it's hilarious to say something like, "Trust me. It's not the clothes. You look fat naked too." But most guys know better. (You can tell the ones who've learned this through trial and error by the permanent frying pan dents in their foreheads!) So you know *that's* not "The Right Answer™", but what is?

You think she wants to know if the outfit she has on is showing the few extra pounds she's carrying, right? WRONG! Here's the secret. She's not really asking a question at all. What she's really saying is, "I need to hear that I'm still attractive to you."

So you answer what you THINK is the question, "Do I look fat?"

You say, "Don't be ridiculous," meaning she looks great. Unfortunately, when you say "Don't be ridiculous," she hears, "You're shallow and silly!"

From YOUR point of view she asked you if she looks fat and you told her she looks great. So why is she so mad? Put it together from *her* point of view. She says, "I need to hear that I'm still attractive to you," and you say, "You're shallow and silly!"

When you see it from her (albeit twisted) perspective, you can see why she's hurt and angry by your attempt to tell her she's not fat. *You* know that you're trying to tell her it's a ridiculous notion that she looks fat. That's a compliment right? Wrong.

You forgot to "translate" and answer what she *really* said. Remember, in her mind she asked you to tell her she's attractive and you called her silly. SLAM!

I know exactly what you're thinking. Geez, translating her question to figure out what she's really asking for and then giving the right answer sounds like a lot of work. Why doesn't she just say what she needs in the first place? Heck, I don't know. Chances are even *she* doesn't know what her "real" question is at the time. But it doesn't really matter.

This is the way women speak and frankly it's not going to change in your lifetime so you might as well learn to work with it. Instead of wishing that women would be more direct, if you ever hope to have a relationship where sex is plentiful and slammed doors are few and far between, I suggest you take just a few minutes and learn the secret I have to offer. I promise, it's not tough at all!

In fact, it's totally worth it because by learning to "translate" you'll avoid a lot of longer discussions filled with even more questions. Read the examples in this book. A lot of them will sound very familiar to you. As you read, pretty soon you'll become very good at translating your lady's questions.

And figuring out what she's really looking for couldn't be easier! In *every one* of the examples in this book, you'll notice that all those impossible questions are *always* asking for the same thing—reassurance.

The bottom line is that a red flag should go up when you find yourself asking, "What the heck does she want from me?" Here's the answer *every time*: She needs your reassurance. And that impossible question she's asking will give you the clue as to what she needs reassurance about.

I'm sure you might think the answers I give you in the coming chapters may sound corny and that she'd never accept them coming from you. But I guarantee that, delivered correctly, they'll work magic! Initially your lady may be a bit suspicious. After all, from her perspective you've been kind of a jerk. Multiply the situation we talked about a moment ago ("Tell me I'm still attractive to you" — "You're silly and shallow") by hundreds of times and you'll see why she feels that way.

But keep it up for a while and you'll be stunned how, after reassuring her with the right answer, she'll smile happily and move on with what she was doing. No more crazy reactions to your "reasonable" responses. No more slammed doors. You'll have a contented lady who got what she needed from you and is ready to let you get back to the game. Now isn't that prospect worth reading a few pages for?

Here's what you'll find in the following chapters. First, a bit of lighthearted advice on the subject that chapter covers. Then, example questions with a translation of what she really means with the question. Then you'll see the wrong answers followed by what you might find as a very surprising translation of what she hears when you give the wrong answer. Finally, you will see the right answer in bold followed by what she hears when you give the right answer. Please resist the urge to only read the question and the right answer. Understanding what it is she is hearing is critical to this book being helpful to you.

Do I look fat in this?

> Translation: I need to hear that I'm attractive to you.

> Wrong answer: Don't be ridiculous. (Or any of the so called "funny" responses mentioned above.)

> She hears: You're shallow and silly.

> **Right answer: Hey, you look great in that, in anything, and in nothing! (Give her a wink.)**

> She hears: I think you look great and I want you. (She's reassured.)

Finally, the questions will be followed by a brief summary which is "the bottom line" on that subject.

As you read this book and the typical wrong answers that guys give, you might think to yourself, *"I'd never say something like that!"* But you'd be surprised. Often guys, who are aware they give the wrong answer occasionally, don't realize how often they do it. Here's a test to tell if you're one of those guys who is always getting it wrong:

Pretend to see an article in the paper or on-line and say to your lady, "Wow. Here's another story about a beautiful actress marrying one of those dumb athletes who can't seem to say anything right. All the biggest jerks get the most beautiful women."

If your lady responds with, "Thank you!" then you definitely need to read the following chapters. The good news is that you were smart enough to buy this book. And if a woman has given it to you, clearly you'll benefit from it.

So as you find yourself denying you're like the guys who answered the "wrong way", it's time for a reality check. The wrong answers in this book came from actual answers guys have given to women. In other words, I couldn't make this stuff up!

Enough with all these explanations, here are the right answers...

Chapter 2

<u>Questions About How She Looks</u>

Let's face it, questions about how a woman looks torment guys the most or at least the most often. Our title question of "Do I look fat in this?" is such a landmine for guys that it's become a running joke. And frankly, women ask a lot of these types of questions. And more frankly, you guys really hate it!

I've heard a lot of what are meant to be funny responses to that question. One is:

"Do these pants make me look fat?"—"No, your big butt makes you look fat."

You guys think these kinds of remarks are so clever. But if you'd ever stop laughing long enough, you'd notice that women aren't laughing at all.

Tom Wilson, the creator of "Ziggy" cartoons, once said, "Wisdom doesn't necessarily come with age. Sometimes age just shows up all by itself." Well that's certainly true when it comes to guys understanding women. Even most of the oldest men on the planet haven't figured this one out yet. So let me just flat out tell you.

Whenever a woman asks a guy any question about how she looks, or how she used to look, or how she may look when she's older, she wants one thing. She wants her guy to tell her she's attractive to him regardless of her age or how many times he's said it to her before. That's it. It's that simple. She doesn't really care if she's gained a few pounds or if her highlights are growing out or any of that. What matters to her is that her guy finds her attractive and that he's proud to be seen with her.

Tip: Don't give commentary, offer reassurance!

Which shoes should I wear with this outfit?

Translation: I want you to pay attention to me and care about how I look.

Wrong answer: Either is fine. It doesn't matter.

She hears: I don't care about you or how you look.

Right answer: (Pause, pretend to care deeply, and point at one then say...) Those, I think. (She'll pick the ones she likes best anyway!)

She hears: I'm paying attention and care about you and what's important to you. (She's reassured.)

Do you wish I was still as thin as when we first met?

Translation: I need to know you still love me and find me attractive.

Wrong answer: Your health would be better if you lost a few pounds. (She already knows this!)

She hears: You're fat and I'd love you more if you were skinnier.

Right answer: You look better to me now than you ever have. (Smile and swat her gently on the bottom.)

She hears: I love you just the way you are. (She's reassured.)

Do I look better with long hair or short hair (or as a brunette or a blonde, etc.)?

Translation: I need to hear that my hair is appealing and sexy to you.

Wrong answer: It doesn't matter—either way.

She hears: Your hair doesn't interest me and therefore neither do you.

Right answer: You're one of those rare ladies who look really sexy either way! (Hug her and then smell and stroke her hair.)

She hears: You're very attractive to me in any hairstyle. (She's reassured.)

Should I get breast implants?

Translation: I need to know you like my breasts.

Wrong answer: If you'd feel better about yourself, go ahead. (Or worse, trying to be funny—"Cool! That'd be great!" Or even worse than that, being serious, "Cool! That'd be great!")

She hears: I don't like your breasts.

Right answer: Why would you even consider messing with perfection?

She hears: Your breasts are very sexy to me. (She's reassured.)

Do you think I dress sexy enough (or too sexy)?

Translation: I want to know if you're proud of me when we're together in public.

Wrong answer: You dress fine. (Or any answer involving librarians or strippers!)

She hears: I don't even look at you anymore. (Or I'm embarrassed by you in public.)

Right answer: You dress perfectly. Heck, everywhere we go I keep hoping to run into my old high school classmates so they can see the catch I landed!

She hears: I think you look great and I'm very proud to be seen with you. (She's reassured.)

Would you say my build is curvy or athletic?

Translation: I need to know you find my body sexy.

Wrong answer: (Saying either "curvy" or "athletic" or any other commentary on those words.)

She hears: (You can't win with either word. If you answer with "curvy" she'll hear fat. If you answer "athletic" she'll hear muscular or butch.)

Right answer: I don't know what they call it, but it sure does it for me! (Raise your eyebrows a few times to indicate a lecherous thought.)

She hears: You're very sexy to me. (She's reassured.)

Don't you wish I could still wear a bikini?

Translation: I need to hear my body is sexy enough for you.

Wrong answer: (Scared of the question you may try to deflect it with humor...) Well technically you could... but I think that ship has sailed don't you?

She hears: Yes, you're fat. But I'm too nervous to say it so I'll joke about it.

Right answer: It's not the paint job baby; it's the performance that counts. And when it comes to pleasing me, you're my NASCAR champion in bed!

She hears: I enjoy sex with you very much even if you don't look like a Playboy bunny or the babysitter. (She's reassured.)

Do you care if I go without make-up today?

Translation: I need to know that you consider me pretty without trying.

Wrong answer: Whatever.
She hears: I don't care either way because I hardly look at you.

Right answer: You always look great with or without make-up. Skip it today and I'll be seen with my natural beauty.

She hears: You don't have to go to any trouble to look great. (She's reassured.)

What the heck am I going to wear to the party?

Translation: I'm concerned I won't look good at the party.

Wrong answer: Geez, you have so many clothes, there's no way you don't have anything to wear.

She hears: You're being unrealistic and it doesn't matter to me how you look or feel.

Right answer: You look sexy in everything you have! But maybe the party's a great excuse to get something new. (Listen, she's going to go out and buy it anyway. You might as well get credit for suggesting it!)

She hears: Your feelings matter to me and I'm willing to spend money to see that you're happy. (She's reassured.)

Don't you think I'm starting to look just like my mother?

Translation: I'm scared that my best days are behind me.

Wrong answer: What'd you expect? (Or trying to be nice, saying just "No" which means to her that you don't want to talk to her.)

She hears: You look old because you are old.

Right answer: You have her same beautiful (eyes, hair, skin, etc.). But other than that, I don't really see it. You're much prettier.

She hears: You got the very best features of your mother but otherwise you're uniquely good-looking. (She's reassured.)

The bottom line on questions about how she looks: If a woman asks you any impossible question that has anything at all to do with how she used to, currently, or is going to look—don't actually answer the question! Just reassure her that she looks absolutely terrific and that you are proud to be seen with her.

Chapter 3

<u>Questions About the Future</u>

> Her: "I loved it when we first got together and we'd sit and ask each other never-ending questions about the future we hoped to have together. Can you say the same thing?"
>
> Him: "I can... but not with a straight face."

You guys seem to be especially frustrated by a woman's questions about the future because you think women are actually seeking information about what's going to happen. You think, "I don't have a crystal ball! Why are you asking me?"

Well the answer's simple. She isn't seeking information about what's going to happen. She's seeking reassurance. She just wants to know that everything's going to be okay. When she asks an impossible question about the future, it means she's feeling unsure—unsure of herself, unsure of the two of you as a couple, unsure of whatever it is she's asking about.

For guys this makes about as much sense as this scenario:

> A man's driving down the highway and his car engine suddenly begins making a horrendous noise. As it

grinds, shimmies, and sputters, he pulls over, hops out, and throws up the hood. Rather than look around to figure out what's wrong and fix it, instead he looks deep into the engine and says, "Listen car, I know how you feel. It's tough riding down this highway mile after mile. But we're in this together and we're going to do just fine." Then he drops the hood, hops back in the car, and turns the key. The engine starts easily, runs smoothly, and then continues on down the road without a single indication of having had any mechanical trouble at all.

Now that scene may sound nuts to you guys. But as much as you like to think of your cars as "she", machines and women couldn't be more different. Unlike that high performance car, what's bothering a woman can very often be fixed with nothing more than encouraging words.

So when you get frustrated when a woman asks you impossible questions about the future regarding things you couldn't possibly predict, notice this: In all the translations of women's questions above, and in all those in all the chapters to follow, the translation doesn't come out as a question at all. In other words, she's not really asking a question and isn't actually seeking information!

What? Her impossible question isn't even a question? That's right! You'll go a very long way with your lady when you learn this secret. Her impossible question is a statement about her feelings and her need for reassurance. So listen to her "question", discern what is troubling her, and then reassure her about that subject. It will work absolute magic! I promise.

Tip: Don't make predictions, offer reassurance!

When will I *finally* get a promotion?

> Translation: I've worked very hard and I need to hear I'll achieve my goals.

Wrong answer: How should I know? I don't work there.

She hears: Why are you annoying me about something I have no control over?

Right answer: You're amazing at what you do! I'm absolutely sure it won't be long before it happens.

She hears: You're worthy of the promotion and will absolutely get it. Hang in there. (She's reassured.)

Do you think we'll be invited to the wedding?

Translation: I'm worried we may not be a couple that people want to socialize with.

Wrong answer: Frankly, I don't really care either way.

She hears: I don't care about the things that matter to you.

Right answer: If they don't, they'll miss out on the most interesting people they could include! I know—let's check out that new restaurant if we're free that night.

She hears: We're undoubtedly wonderful company and we can have a good time regardless. (She's reassured.)

How many kids do you think we'll have?

Translation: I need to know that, like me, you sometimes dream about what our future will look like.

Wrong answer: Who can afford kids these days?

She hears: None of your dreams will come true and our future is basically pretty bleak.

Right answer: That will be an exciting time, huh? I was thinking two or three. How many do you want?

She hears: I've thought about this and I'm excited about that stage of our lives. It matters to me too. (She's reassured.)

Is this new recipe going to turn out okay?

Translation: I've worked hard on this and I'm concerned it might taste awful and you'll think I'm a bad cook.

Wrong answer: (Trying to be funny...) If not, you just blew twenty bucks.

She hears: I care more about money than your efforts to please me.

Right answer: It's going to be great! You're a wonderful cook. I can't wait to taste it.

She hears: I'm on your side and I have confidence in your abilities. (She's reassured.)

Do you think the new neighbors will like us?

Translation: It's important to me that we're liked and I need to hear we're worthy of other people's approval.

Wrong answer: Why do you always make yourself miserable caring what people think?

She hears: You're weak and lack the confidence I have.

Right answer: I'm sure they will! We always make friends everywhere we go.

She hears: I care too and I'm confident we're worthy of anyone's friendship. (She's reassured.)

Am I going to pass my final exams?

Translation: I'm worried that no matter how much I study I may still not do well.

Wrong answer: Sure. Why wouldn't you?

She hears: I'm oblivious to your deepest fears and concerns.

Right answer: You're smart and you're prepared. Not only will you pass, but you'll pass with flying colors. You'll be the curve buster!

She hears: I have total faith in you and your abilities. (She's reassured.)

Do you think the kids will get into college?

Translation: I'm very uneasy about our kids' futures.

Wrong answer: The kids are only in grade school. Geez, why are you worrying about that now?

She hears: You're irrational and you always go looking for trouble.

Right answer: Absolutely! We're doing all the right things to be sure they're prepared to do really well. They'll get in.

She hears: Don't worry. Our kids have bright futures. (She's reassured.)

Will we ever find someone we trust to watch the baby when I go back to work?

Translation: I'm feeling extremely anxious about finding a good caregiver.

Wrong answer: That's kind of your department.

She hears: I'm not very concerned about who takes care of our baby and so I'm not going to be a part of the decision making.

Right answer: Yeah, it's important we find just the right person! We just won't quit looking until we find someone we both feel really good about.

She hears: Like you, I see this as critical and I'm with you in this very important search. (She's reassured.)

What if no one wants to buy my crafts?

Translation: I need to hear that my creations are worthwhile (and therefore *I'm* worthwhile).

Wrong answer: Well, it's just a hobby. I don't really get why you're doing this anyway.

She hears: I think your crafts are silly and a waste of time.

Right answer: Your crafts are amazing! I think if you'll find just the right place to sell them, they'll be a huge hit.

She hears: You, and how you spend your time, matter to me. I think you're great! (She's reassured.)

Do you think it will rain on our barbeque next month?

Translation: I've worked hard putting this together and I'm worried about what I can't control.

Wrong answer: Either it will or it won't. How should I know?

She hears: I really don't care if the special day you've worked so hard on is ruined.

Right answer: I don't think it will. I really don't. But if it does, we'll figure it out. It's going to be a great day. I can't wait! (Smile at her.)

She hears: Don't worry. And if your fears come true I'm here to help you. (She's reassured.)

The bottom line on questions about the future: If a woman asks you any impossible question that has anything at all to do with the future—don't actually answer the question! She's feeling unsure about the future. Just reassure her that she's capable, that you guys are strong as a couple and will face things together, and that the future is bright!

Chapter 4

Questions About the Past

When a woman asks you a question about the past, you guys feel like you've just landed in the middle of a high-stakes pop quiz. Admit it. She asks you a question about your past together and suddenly you rack your brain for the details while the theme from Jeopardy starts playing inside your head. When you can't come up with anything, you're sure that the buzzer will go off, sending you to the couch with your pillow and blanket in tow where you'll sleep until your ears are hairier than the top of your head. All in all, not a great experience.

One reason you guys worry about questions about the past is because you know that women remember the details of the past so much better than you do.

> Her: "Honey, I love that you've always been there for me. Do you remember back when we first met and I twisted my ankle and you carried me all the way home?"

> Him: "Not really... but if you say so."

> Her again: "What about that time we went on a picnic and I was stung by a wasp? I was so glad you were there to hold ice on my back. Remember that?"

Him again: "No... can't say I do."

Her again: "Oh honey, but surely you remember when we were bike riding and I got that flat tire and you were there to fix it for me?"

Him: "I'm really trying. But I don't remember that either."

Her: "Never mind. It's finally dawned on me... you're bad luck!"

But you guys wouldn't work so hard to remember those blasted details if you knew she's not checking your memory at all! When she asks you one of those "Do you remember when..." questions, she's either second guessing herself about a decision she's made or she needs reassurance that your shared history is important to you.

So don't hurt yourself trying to come up with details. They don't matter! You just need to say something that will make her understand that your history together means a lot to you!

Tip: Don't try to remember, offer reassurance!

Do you remember what I wore on our first date?

Translation: Show me that you remember our early days because it will let me know that I'm important to you.

Wrong answer: Heck, I don't even remember what you wore yesterday—I've slept since then.

She hears: You're not important to me.

Right answer: I don't remember exactly what you were wearing but I *do* remember that

you looked absolutely beautiful. (Take her in your arms.)

She hears: You still have me in your spell and I'm still yours. (She's reassured.)

Do you think my mom was upset that we didn't spend the holidays at her house?

Translation: I really don't want my mother upset with us.

Wrong answer: Well, she'll just have to deal with it! It's only fair that we finally spent Christmas with my family for a change.

She hears: I don't care if your mother is mad at us and neither should you.

Right answer: I know she was disappointed. Isn't it funny how, even as adults, we still care so much about pleasing our parents?

She hears: I understand your mom's unhappy. But you're an adult and shouldn't feel pressured by her. I'm here for you and we'll face her reaction together. (She's reassured.)

Did we miss our chance to travel before the kids came along?

Translation: I'm troubled about whether we'll ever really get to live out the dreams we have.

Wrong answer: You're the one who was in such a rush to have a baby!

She hears: You have no right to regret because you called the shots about starting a family.

Right answer: They're getting bigger every day and they'll be off to college before we know it. And we'll still be young enough to take all the trips we've talked about.

She hears: I still believe we will do all the wonderful things we've dreamed of doing. (She's reassured.)

Do you remember those boots I liked so much?

Translation: Prove you were paying attention when we were shopping because it tells me you care about me.

Wrong answer: What boots?

She hears: I didn't pay attention because I don't care about what you like.

Right answer: I remember the way your face lit up when you told me you liked them but I don't actually remember the boots.

She hears: I'm paying attention to your face and enjoy seeing you happy. But I'm going to be truthful about not remembering details of shopping. (She's reassured.)

Why didn't I go see my dad when he got sick?

Translation: I feel like I'm a terrible person because I didn't go to see my dad one last time.

Wrong answer: Don't worry about it. He was so out of it he didn't know the difference.

She hears: Be like me and don't do anything difficult or unpleasant when you can find an excuse not to.

Right answer: Everyone knows you would have been there if there was any way possible. Besides, your prayers for him could be heard from right here and that's what he really needed most at the time.

She hears: You have nothing to regret. You did everything you could and that makes you a good person. (She's reassured.)

Remember the day when Junior was born?

Translation: Show me that the meaningful days in our lives are as important to you as they are to me.

Wrong answer: I missed a whole night's sleep waiting for him to be born. That day's just a foggy blur.

She hears: Sleep matters more to me than our son's birth.

Right answer: Yeah. He sure kept us waiting, huh? I think we went through three full shifts of nurses before he finally came.

She hears: That day matters greatly to me and I enjoy reminiscing with you. (She's reassured.)

Why didn't we buy the house on the corner that we liked so much?

Translation: I'm concerned that we may have made a big mistake in the house we chose.

Wrong answer: You've got to be kidding me! You're the one who said it was too big to clean.

She hears: We should have bought it but you were against it. We made a mistake and it's your fault.

Right answer: I love our house! Besides, that one seemed really too big, remember? I know we made the right choice.

She hears: We made the decision jointly and we made the right decision. (She's reassured.)

What was that song you used to sing to me?

Translation: I miss those times when you were very romantic and I wonder if you still love me as much as you did back then.

Wrong answer: I don't know. That was a long time ago.

She hears: Those times are not important to me and you should not expect to ever see that kind of romance again.

Right answer: Oh yeah... what was that song? If you help me remember it, I'll try to sing it to you right now.

She hears: The time when we were falling in love is special to me and I want to keep those memories and that romance alive. (She's reassured.)

Was I wrong to tell my sister to back off?

Translation: I'm worried that I have seriously alienated someone I love.

Wrong answer: Absolutely not! She had it coming.

She hears: Viciously cut people out of your life if they cross you. (And be careful because I may do the same to you some day.)

Right answer: I know it's hard when you and your sister aren't speaking. But after she

considers what you said, you guys will have an even better relationship.

She hears: I know you're worried and miss her but you did the right thing. You two will be best friends again soon. (She's reassured.)

What did you notice first about me when we met?

Translation: I need to hear something you like about me.

Wrong answer: I remember that tight little skirt you had on.

She hears: I first sized you up as an easy mark for sex.

Right answer: First? Either your eyes or your hair I guess. But I remember when we talked, thinking you were so kind and intelligent. But I have to admit your gorgeous eyes drew me in first.

She hears: I loved and still love your eyes and I was drawn to you by your wonderful personality. (She's reassured.)

The bottom line on questions about the past: If a woman asks you any impossible question that has anything at all to do with the past—she's not testing you. She's either feeling insecure about past decisions or she wants to know if your shared history is important to you. Remember, you don't actually have to answer the question! Just reassure her that you've both made good decisions and that you remember your times together very fondly (if not in detail).

Chapter 5

<u>Questions About</u>
<u>Her Friends and Family</u>

A man noticed an unusual funeral procession approaching; a long black hearse, followed by a second long black hearse, followed by a limo, followed by a man walking a mean looking dog on a leash, followed finally by a long line of about 200 men walking single file. The man couldn't stand his curiosity.

He respectfully approached the guy walking the dog and said, "I'm so sorry for your loss, and I know now is a bad time to disturb you, but I've never seen a funeral procession like this. Whose funeral is it?"

The guy replied, "Well, in that first hearse is my mother-in-law. She was attacked and killed by this dog. In the second hearse is my brother-in-law who tried to help her and was also attacked and killed by my dog. In the limo is my wife."

After a thoughtful moment of silence passed, the man asked, "Can I borrow the dog?"

The answer..."Get in line."

Okay, so your lady's family members aren't necessarily your favorite people. Sometimes you have the urge to remind her

28

that you chose her, you didn't choose them. But face it, they're a package deal.

We've been through several chapters of questions now, so you should know that when a woman asks you impossible questions about her family she doesn't really want your advice. She's seeking reassurance! And as you've probably also figured out, friends are extremely important to a woman as well.

> Woman: "My best friend ran away with my husband. It's only been three days and I already really miss her!"

As with all humor, there's a grain of truth to that. And when things are not going well with her friends, a woman's going to ask *you* a lot of impossible questions—even more so than usual I'm afraid.

If you've read each of the previous chapters and read through all the questions and answers, you should be getting the idea by now. When a woman asks you an impossible question about her family or friends, remember to...

> Stop... Think... and Translate!

The actual question should not be answered. It's only a clue! The impossible question is merely a guidepost to point you towards what it is she's seeking reassurance about.

Tip: Don't furnish advice, offer reassurance!

Are you looking forward to my mother's visit?

> Translation: I need to hear that you aren't too annoyed about her upcoming visit and that you love me enough to put up with her.

> Wrong answer: Is she coming AGAIN!?

She hears: I hate your mother and don't want to put up with her even to please you.

Right answer: I hate sharing you with anyone but since she IS your mom, I guess I can be generous for a little while. (Wink at her)

She hears: I love being with you and will make sacrifices for you. (She's reassured.)

Do you like my best friend?

Translation: I chose my friend because I admire her qualities and want you to like her too.

Wrong answer: Sure. Why not?

She hears: I'm barely listening and I don't want to give your questions real thought.

Right answer: Like you, she's intelligent and has a big heart. She's the perfect best friend for you.

She hears: You're a good person and you made a great choice in picking your friend. (She's reassured.)

I can't believe she said that about me. Can you?

Translation: I'm hurt and need you to rally around me now.

Wrong answer: You shouldn't be surprised. She's always been like that.

She hears: You make terrible choices in those you build relationships with and so you deserve to be hurting now.

Right answer: I know it hurts when someone you care for is cruel like that. But it's not really like her, is it? You guys need to talk.

She hears: I'm with you. I care that you are hurting. I support the relationship. (She's reassured.)

(Crying) So should I just quit my book group?

Translation: I really don't want to quit but something's bothering me deeply.

Wrong answer: If it makes you cry like this, then you ought to just quit.

She hears: I don't care what's wrong I just want you to stop crying.

Right answer: You wouldn't be crying if your book group didn't mean a lot to you. I think you guys all need to talk.

She hears: I recognize what and who is important to you and I support your efforts to maintain those relationships. (She's reassured.)

Why didn't my friends include me when they all went out last night?

Translation: I'm feeling really left out and hurt by my friends.

Wrong answer: Why do you care? Besides, we can't afford for you to be blowing money eating out anyway.

She hears: You're weak for caring and money's more important than your feelings.

Right answer: I'm not sure. But hey, we all sometimes forget to include people we really

care about. I'm sure they just forgot. Give them a call and check it out.

She hears: You're worthy and I'm sure it was just an oversight. I encourage you to reconnect so you'll feel better. (She's reassured.)

How come she ignored my friend request on Facebook?

Translation: I think I'm being snubbed by someone I reached out to.

Wrong answer: Why do you assume she even saw it? You always think the worst.

She hears: You're a negative person. No wonder she blew you off.

Right answer: You're a great person! I'm sure anyone would love to get a friend request from you. Some people don't get on their Facebook accounts very often.

She hears: You're someone people like. I'm sure you'll get your request accepted soon. (She's reassured.)

I swear, I don't think I'll ever be able to please my dad, you know?

Translation: I'm feeling unworthy because my father doesn't offer his approval.

Wrong answer: Look, he's impossible to please so you might as well quit trying.

She hears: You're right. You'll never please him.

Right answer: His generation is different. I think he's very proud of you just as you are,

even if he doesn't show it in a way we really understand.

She hears: You have his approval and you should not feel unworthy. (She's reassured.)

Why do I always seem to end up in the middle of their fights with each other?

Translation: I'm weary of playing referee and want to know if my involvement even makes a difference.

Wrong answer: See? I've told you to just stay out of it. Sometimes I think you just like being in the middle of their drama.

She hears: You're a meddler who won't take my good advice. Your involvement in their fights is to entertain yourself and is annoying to me.

Right answer: You're a natural mediator. They turn to you because you make a difference. I'm sure they're glad you're willing to help. If they aren't, they should be.

She hears: You're important and you're helping people. (She's reassured.)

My mother just won't hear me. Why does she keep doing the same thing over and over?

Translation: I feel helpless in communicating with my mother.

Wrong answer: She hears you. She's just stubborn. You know that.

She hears: Don't bother trying to tell her anything because your mother is a terrible person who will always be a thorn in your side.

Right answer: It's frustrating I know. Maybe we need to work harder to arrange things so that her decisions can't really have an impact on our lives.

She hears: I understand you're feeling powerless but I'm in this with you and I'm willing to help seek solutions. (She's reassured.)

Do you think my new friend is really only interested in selling me stuff?

Translation: I'm concerned I'm someone that people might not want to get to know if I have nothing to offer but friendship.

Wrong answer: Probably. She's already asked you to do one of those party things here at the house. I swear, everyone is just out to make a buck these days.

She hears: The only reason someone would be interested in you is if they could make money off you. You are uninteresting and worthless.

Right answer: No way! Just because she does home sales parties doesn't mean she doesn't genuinely like you. Clearly she's got great judgment if she's selected you as a new friend.

She hears: You're a worthwhile and fascinating person. (She's reassured.)

The bottom line on questions about her family and friends: If a woman asks you any impossible question that has anything at all to do with her family or friends—she's not looking for advice on what to do. She's either feeling insecure about how she's handled a relationship or she's not sure about her ability to handle it in the future. Don't actually answer the question! Just reassure her that you understand how important her family and friends are to her and that she has the ability to manage her important relationships skillfully.

Chapter 6

Questions About Your Buddies and Your Family

A guy didn't come home one night. Knowing confession is good for the soul but can be bad for the marriage, the next day he told his wife he'd slept over at a buddy's house. So she called her husband's ten best friends to check out his story. Eight of them confirmed that he'd slept over and the other two of them claimed he was still there.

While funny, this illustrates exactly why your lady asks you a lot of impossible questions about the people who are the key players in your life. She wants to know who you're closest to, who you're relying on, who you tell the truth to, and who, therefore, means the most to you.

Her questions probably feel to you like criticisms of your buddies and family so you tend to get defensive. Deep down, what upsets you is that you really want your lady to approve of the friends you've chosen and the family you haven't. Heck, when you feel like she's being extra disapproving, it seems even your imaginary friends are telling you that you've made a mistake.

But your lady isn't nearly as condemning of your friends and family as it feels. When she asks these, never-ending, impossible questions about them, what she really wants to know is where she fits in. She knows that unless your friend has murdered someone in your immediate family, you're going to rush to bail him out immediately. What she wants to know is would you do the same for her?

When a woman asks you all those impossible questions about your buddies or family, she's really wondering what your priorities are when it comes to pleasing her versus pleasing the others in your life. Every woman wants to be number one in her man's life. And more importantly, once she feels that she comes first, she's willing to let go of a lot.

Tip: Don't get defensive, offer reassurance!

Why don't you care that your brother insulted me?

Translation: I'm hurt and disappointed that you don't seem willing to stand up for me.

Wrong answer: He was drunk. He didn't know what he was saying.

She hears: I don't care if drunken family members are rude to you and I'll stand by and do nothing as long as they have alcohol as an excuse for their behavior.

Right answer: There was no reasoning with him in his condition. I didn't want to cause a scene. I intend to call him and make it very clear that, drunk or sober, he will never treat you that way again!

She hears: I will stand up for you even against my own family members. (She's reassured.)

Why don't you want to tell your parents how serious we are?

Translation: I fear that you're hiding the real depth of our relationship from your family because you secretly suspect it isn't going to work out.

Wrong answer: Why do you keep pushing me about that? I'll tell them when I'm ready.

She hears: You're annoying me so much that I may never tell them since I don't expect to be with you much longer.

Right answer: I guess I'm a little weird about talking to my parents about such personal things. But it doesn't mean I'm not fully committed to you.

She hears: It isn't the level of our relationship that keeps me from discussing it with my parents. It's just that I'm uncomfortable communicating with them. (She's reassured.)

How come you always seem to get drunk when you go out with your buddies?

Translation: I wonder why you're willing to "cut loose" with them but you're more serious with me. I'm also scared that you'll get hurt or do something stupid.

Wrong answer: Not this again! I told you, I've got to have a little fun once in a while. Now get off my case, will you?

She hears: I can't have fun with you and nagging me about drinking with my buddies is further proof of that fact.

Right answer: I never drink and drive, so don't worry. But guys need that locker room stuff just to blow off steam. I'm just cutting up with my friends. You and I do fun stuff too... just a different kind of fun. (Wink at her.)

She hears: I'm safe. I'm just being a guy. I respect you too much to be that way with you. I love you and our time together. (She's reassured.)

Does your sister really expect us to spend the holidays at her house this year?

Translation: I don't want to be forced into celebrating where I don't want to.

Wrong answer: Sometimes I want to be with my family on the holidays too!

She hears: It's not about you; it's about me.

Right answer: I know we have fun with your family and they'll miss us. But my family loves you and wants to see us on the holidays too!

She hears: Your feelings matter to me and my family cares for you and would like to see us. (She's reassured.)

Why do you always want to watch the game with your brothers instead of with me?

Translation: I'm afraid I'm less important to you than I used to be.

Wrong answer: You don't even like football!

She hears: You and I don't have common interests. So you're right. You aren't that important to me anymore.

Right answer: It's only for a few hours and then I'll come right home and we'll have a lot more fun together than the guys and I could ever have!

She hears: You are important to me. (She's reassured.)

Don't you think it looks bad for you to be meeting for coffee with a woman who isn't your wife?

Translation: I'm scared you're vulnerable to having an affair with her.

Wrong answer: Why are you always so jealous? Nothing's going on. I hate it when you try to control me by insinuating something's up.

She hears: This is your problem because I'm going to do whatever I want regardless of how it makes you feel.

Right answer: Everybody knows you're the only woman in the world for me! But to be sure she never gets the wrong idea I'll stick to discussing work related issues only.

She hears: I love only you and care about how you feel. I'll be sure no lines are crossed. (She's reassured.)

Does your best friend think he knows you better than I do just because he's known you longer?

Translation: I want everyone to consider me the world's greatest authority on you.

Wrong answer: Actually, since we were kids together, he probably knows a lot about me that you don't.

She hears: He is more important to me than you are.

Right answer: Nobody in the world could know me better than you do! You and I share a bank account, a bed, and a lot of secrets. Who could know me better than that?

She hears: You're the one person in the world who really knows me deep inside and therefore you're the most important person in my life. (She's reassured.)

Why don't they understand that sometimes we need time alone?

Translation: Please stand up to others in defense of our time alone together.

Wrong answer: Don't go criticizing them again. They're welcome here any time they want to drop by.

She hears: They are more important to me than you are.

Right answer: My time alone with you is very important to me. I don't want you to feel like anyone is intruding on that. Do you want me to talk to them about this?

She hears: You're my priority and I hear your concerns. I'm willing to work to make this better. (She's reassured.)

Why does your mother refuse to call before she comes over?

Translation: Who is your priority; her or me?

Wrong answer: Why does she have to call? I'm her son for goodness sake.

She hears: I won't go up against my mother even at the expense of you feeling she's imposing on us.

Right answer: I know it's important to you so I'll talk to her. But maybe we could just not answer the door if she doesn't call first. I bet she'll learn quickly that way. (Laugh)

She hears: You matter more to me than my mother and we'll work as a team to set boundaries. (She's reassured.)

How come your council meeting has to be at the same time as the recital?

Translation: I want you to skip the meeting and come to the kid's recital.

Wrong answer: Do you realize how nuts that question is? The council can't check the schedules of the kids of every member before setting the date. Besides, this was on the calendar since last year!

She hears: You are crazy and astonishingly unreasonable.

Right answer: I hate these scheduling conflicts too! I'm disappointed. Next time,

when I'm not giving the main presentation, I'll skip the meeting and go to the recital.

She hears: I don't want to miss family events but sometimes I have no control over it. I'm trying not to be too disappointed and I need you to help me with that. (She's reassured.)

The bottom line on questions about your buddies and your family: If a woman asks you any impossible question that has anything at all to do with your buddies or your family—she's not grilling you on your choices or even being critical. She's either feeling insecure about how she fits into your life or she feels threatened by the influence others have on you and on your relationship with her. Don't actually answer her question! Instead, reassure her that she's the most important person in your life and that no one has the power to negatively impact your opinion of her or your feelings for her.

Chapter 7

Questions About the House and Kids

You guys know that most women take their responsibilities as homemakers, and especially as mothers, very seriously. While you may think it's fine to settle important decisions in these areas with rock, paper, scissors, she most likely has a higher standard. Because of this, she'll sometimes feel unsure about past decisions or future abilities and she'll ask you probing and, at times, agonizingly impossible questions about these subjects.

Unless you've jumped ahead and this is literally the first page you've read of this book, by now you know that when women ask these impossible questions they're seeking reassurance. But impossible questions about the house and kids are in a special category. There are actually sort of subcategories on this one. Now don't get all zoned out on me here. I promise this one's easy. Here's the deal...

Even some of you modern-minded guys who believe in equal rights for women secretly maintain a deep-seated belief that the house and the kids are ultimately the responsibility of women. Ironically, some of you think this way because you believe the house and kids represent work that's beneath you.

The rest of you think this way because you're afraid you aren't quite up to the task. Either way, you're wrong.

At the end of the day, women are as emotionally and physically wrung out as the man of the house, and they expect, rightly, that all the chores be shared.

A friend's father used to give him this very sage advice about women: "Son, if you want a thoroughbred, don't treat her like a nag." As a woman, I can't tell you guys how very true that is! Most women respond very positively to being treated well. And that includes feeling that you are willing to lend a hand.

Finally, it's important that you guys recognize that many of the impossible questions women ask regarding the house and kids are actually cries for help with the work. They're still asking for reassurance—reassurance that you'll pitch in! And for the record, shouting at the kids, "Hey, don't make me sell you on Ebay!" is *not* considered help.

**Tip: Don't shirk responsibility, offer
reassurance (and assistance)!**

When are we ever going to get around to all the repairs the house needs?

Translation: I feel anxious when things that require attention are left undone.

Wrong answer: I can either earn a living or be a full-time handyman. I can't do both.

She hears: Yes, the house has gotten away from us. But don't count on me to get it done.

Right answer: Yeah, our to-do list sure has grown lately. But we make a great team. We'll just divide and conquer.

She hears: I agree it's an issue but it will be okay because we're going to work together to solve this. (She's reassured.)

How can you let our son speak to me that way?

Translation: You're not standing up for me and it makes me feel alone.

Wrong answer: You're his parent too. If you don't like the way he's speaking to you, take it up with him yourself.

She hears: You are alone to deal with a defiant son.

Right answer: You're right. It's not okay for him to use that tone with you. I'll speak to him about it right away.

She hears: I'm sorry I missed it and I'm on your side. I'll take care of this. (She's reassured.)

Am I the only one who cares about getting things done around here?

Translation: I feel like you just don't take responsibility and that I'm doing all the work.

Wrong answer: (Sarcastically) I guess so.

She hears: I don't care and I won't help.

Right answer: I care, but maybe just not at the same times or at the same levels that you do. But I'll definitely do my share.

She hears: You're not alone. I'll share in the responsibilities. (She's reassured.)

Will you *please* be sure your mother doesn't give the kids any junk food?

Translation: Show me your loyalty has fully shifted from your mother to me by seeing that the rules we've set for our kids are honored by her.

Wrong answer: Are you nuts? I can't control what my mother feeds the kids!

She hears: I'm going to act like you're crazy and I'm angry because I'm really a mama's boy and I'd rather piss you off than go up against her.

Right answer: I'll definitely let her know that if she wants to take care of her grandchildren, she's going to have to follow our rules.

She hears: My loyalty is with you and I'll back you even at the risk of my mother's displeasure. (She's reassured.)

I just heard immunizations can be dangerous. Did we make a big mistake having the baby get her shots?

Translation: I need to hear we are doing the absolute best thing for our child.

Wrong answer: Why do you believe everything you hear? Besides, it's a little late to worry about that now.

She hears: You're naive and we probably screwed up and hurt the baby. But I'm not concerned about that at all.

Right answer: Wow! That's kind of scary, huh? But I know that the baby's pediatrician came very highly recommended and she'd

never do anything that wasn't good for our child.

She hears: I understand your fears and relate to your protective nature. But we've done the right thing and everything's going to be okay. (She's reassured.)

Will you just do *something* to get the kids to stop fighting once and for all?

Translation: I hate to hear the kids fight, I'm at the end of my rope, and I need your help with this.

Wrong answer: What the heck do you expect me to do? They're kids!

She hears: I'm not going to do anything to help. Besides this is an unsolvable problem.

Right answer: I know it's hard to listen to them fight. I'll see what I can do to quiet them down for now. But I have the feeling we're going to have to do it a few million more times in the next couple of years. (Try to chuckle.)

She hears: I understand your frustration and I'm going to help. (She's reassured.)

With so much to do around here, are you seriously going to be on that computer all day?

Translation: I feel like you're wasting your time while I work hard.

Wrong answer: No. I'm not going to do it seriously. I'm going to do it humorously!

She hears: Your concerns about how I spend my time are a joke to me.

Right answer: I know you're getting a lot done right now and I appreciate it. But I'd like to relax for a while. In half an hour I'll check in with you to see how I can help.

She hears: I recognize you're working harder than me right now, but I intend to help soon. (She's reassured.)

Why do I always have to be the bad guy with the kids?

Translation: I feel totally alone in the disciplinary efforts with the kids.

Wrong answer: (Smiling) Because it's my decade to be the good cop.

She hears: Don't count on any help from me.

Right answer: I'm sorry I've left you hanging on that one. From here on I'll do my share of the dirty work.

She hears: I hear you and I'm willing to help. (She's reassured.)

I can't believe you missed the parent-teacher conferences again. Don't you care about our kids' education at all?

Translation: I felt very alone as a parent when I had to meet the children's teachers without you.

Wrong answer: I can't skip work for everything that goes on at that school. Somebody has to support this family!

She hears: You expect too much of me and you're on your own on this one.

Right answer: I really wish I could have been there but I'm glad you do such a great job staying in touch with the kids' teachers. So what'd they have to say?

She hears: I care about the kids and appreciate what you do for them. I want to be involved but for now it will have to be through you. (She's reassured.)

I can't believe I yelled like that! Am I a terrible mom?

Translation: I feel like a terrible mother and I need you to tell me I'm not.

Wrong answer: Geez, I'm telling you... You've got to hold your temper!

She hears: Yes, you are a terrible mother.

Right answer: Listen, even the best moms in the world have moments they aren't proud of. But you're a great mom and the kids will forget it soon. It's nothing to beat yourself up about.

She hears: You're a great mom and this is a trivial matter. (She's reassured.)

Have you ever once helped the kids with their homework?

Translation: I need you to pitch in more with the kids' schoolwork.

Wrong answer: That's your department.

She hears: Don't expect me to pitch in with the kids' schoolwork.

Right answer: Good point. I guess it's never occurred to me to do that. I can take a look at it tonight if you'd like.

She hears: I'm willing to pitch in more with the kids' schoolwork. (She's reassured.)

The bottom line on questions about the house and kids: If a woman asks you any impossible question that has anything at all to do with the house and kids, she's asking for reassurance—one of two kinds. She's asking for your reassurance that she's made good decisions as a mother and that she will continue to do so. Or she's asking for your reassurance that you will pitch in and help. Don't actually answer the question! Instead, reassure her that she has been, is, and will be a good mother and that you're willing to do your share of the work around the house and with the kids. (And then follow through!)

Chapter 8

<u>Questions About</u>
<u>Money and Jobs</u>

Despite the cost of living, it still remains popular. So jobs, and the money they bring, are an important topic for a man and woman who are building a life together. They say that two can live as cheaply as one. What they don't say is that they can only do it half as long. In other words, finances are critical.

And the impossible questions women ask about jobs and money can cause a lot of bickering. Certainly these subjects can be a source of anxiety. But when a woman asks impossible questions about these things, she doesn't want to be given advice like she's a child. What she needs is reassurance that her fretting about these issues is needless and that all will be well.

Sometimes your lady, in an attempt to ease her own worries, will ask impossible questions that feel like she's trying to control you. An example would be our first question below, "Why don't you just tell your boss you aren't going to do it?" The truth is she *is* trying to control; but not so much you, as the situation. You'd be surprised how, offered reassurance, a woman will take comfort, relax, and will let go of that need to control.

At times, women will ask a lot of questions regarding money, jobs, and the decisions being made about these things. Especially if the woman isn't in charge of the family finances, she'll ask questions for reassurance that good decisions are being made. But all those impossible questions can really make a guy feel second-guessed. You know why God created man first don't you? Because he didn't want a bunch of questions while he worked!

What also drives a lot of the conflict about money and jobs is that when women ask questions, you guys tend to respond as if you *always* know best. When a guy is dismissive of a woman and insists he has all the answers, it angers and frustrates the woman who then retaliates with further impossible questions. This tends to escalate the entire debate.

The bickering would decrease tremendously if you guys would understand that, while women will sometimes express concern about money or jobs, they're also equally capable adults. Don't let a woman's impossible questions feel to you like either surrender or an attack. If you'll recognize the questions for what they are, a call for reassurance, and respond correctly, you'll be astonished at not only how well the conversation goes, but how quickly it ends.

Tip: Don't be a know-it-all, offer reassurance!

Why don't you just tell your boss you aren't going to do it?

Translation: I'd like you to stand up for yourself.

Wrong answer: Great, I've got him bossing me around and now you're telling me what to do too. Back off will you?

She hears: I won't listen to anyone.

Right answer: I know it might seem to you like I'm being taken advantage of but I'd never let that happen. I promise I'll take care of it.

She hears: I'm standing up for myself and for us. Trust me to handle things at work. (She's reassured.)

Are we going to be able to afford a vacation this summer?

Translation: I really hope we can go on vacation together.

Wrong answer: I don't know.

She hears: I don't care.

Right answer: I sure hope so! I'd love nothing more than to get away with you. Let's do our best to keep saving.

She hears: I want to go on vacation too and I want us to work together to make it happen. (She's reassured.)

Why do you always blow money we don't have on stuff like that?

Translation: I think you're irresponsible in your spending.

Wrong answer: Hey, I earned it so it's mine to spend.

She hears: I'll be irresponsible if I want to. Besides, it's my money.

Right answer: I know we're on a tight budget but I'm watching what I spend. Besides,

we've planned for money in the budget for each of us to be a little bit frivolous *sometimes*.

She hears: I'm aware of our budgetary restrictions and I spent the money with that issue in mind. I'll be careful with our money. (She's reassured.)

My new boss is seriously crazy. Do you think I should just quit?

Translation: I'm very unhappy at work and want your input.

Wrong answer: You're always talking about quitting! If you're going to do it, just do it already.

She hears: Quit whining. Do whatever you want, but I really don't want to hear about your job anymore.

Right answer: He sure can be very difficult and I know it's tough on you. Are you seriously considering quitting or do you just need to let off steam?

She hears: I'm sympathetic to what you're going through and I'm here to listen. (She's reassured.)

I think the other salesman from your company is selling in your territory. Why don't you call him on it?

Translation: I'm worried about money and want you to be more aggressive at work.

Wrong answer: Why don't you just let me take care of my job, huh?

She hears: I have no clue how I'm going to handle this, but you'd better back off.

Right answer: I know you feel very protective of me and I appreciate it. But I'm keeping a close eye on the situation and I won't let that guy step on my toes.

She hears: I'm taking care of business. (She's reassured.)

Why can't we save any money?

Translation: I'm worried about our financial future.

Wrong answer: Because you spend it all!

She hears: We're broke because of you.

Right answer: We could definitely be doing better. Maybe we need to put a good plan in place. Want to put one together?

She hears: I'm aware of the situation and want to work together to make it better. (She's reassured.)

My sister needs a loan again. You don't mind, do you?

Translation: I'm giving my sister some money and I'm asking you not to be upset with me about it.

Wrong answer: Yes I mind! Your sister needs to learn to manage her money better so she won't always be relying on others to get her out of these pinches.

She hears: Money matters more to me than your relationship with your sister.

Right answer: Because I love you, I'm happy to help out again. But as much as I wish we did, we don't have an endless supply of

money. So we'll have to put some limits on your sister's borrowing.

She hears: Because I love you, it's okay this time. But this is going to have to stop. (She's reassured.)

Do you think it was stupid of me to lock-in a two year cell phone plan?

Translation: I'm second guessing myself and I need to hear I made a good financial decision.

Wrong answer: Why sweat over it now? What's done is done.

She hears: You screwed up and it can't be fixed now.

Right answer: I know how you feel. After I make a decision like that I always have the urge to keep shopping around. But I'm sure you got the best deal there is. (Listen guys, whether it's true or not, there's nothing to be gained by saying otherwise now.)

She hears: I feel like that too sometimes but, don't worry, you did great. (She's reassured.)

When do you think you'll get that raise?

Translation: I'm worried about money.

Wrong answer: I wish I knew.

She hears: I'm out of touch at work and I'm not comfortable checking into whether I'll be getting a raise soon or not.

Right answer: We sure could use it, huh? I'm certainly doing everything I can to make it happen as soon as possible!

She hears: I'm aware of our need for money and I'm working hard to improve our situation. (She's reassured.)

It isn't right that you have to work the weekend again. Can't someone else just take care of it?

Translation: I miss you and I think they're taking advantage of you at work.

Wrong answer: If you had it your way, I'd be the only guy never pulling weekend duty. How would that be fair?

She hears: I'm being responsible and, as usual, your expectations are unreasonable.

Right answer: It may feel like I do more than my share of overtime. But everyone else is on the rotation and unfortunately it's my turn again. I miss you and hate missing fun times. But let's focus on the extra income... it'll sure come in handy!

She hears: I agree it's frustrating but the system's fair and it's my turn again. I miss you too but the money is important. (She's reassured.)

The bottom line on questions about money and jobs: If a woman asks you any impossible question that has anything at all to do with money or jobs, she's asking for reassurance. Don't answer the question! When she asks about money, she wants to hear she's made good financial decisions, she's a good money manager, the two of you are currently in stable financial shape, or that your future is secure. When she asks about jobs, she wants to know that you've got a good handle on your job and that her work is worthwhile.

Chapter 9

<u>Questions About Sex</u>

Guys love to talk about sex. And guys love to talk with women about sex. They say when a guy talks about sex to a woman, it's sexual harassment. And when a woman talks about sex to a guy, it's $4.95 a minute.

But seriously, when in the middle of playful pillow talk a guy suddenly finds himself under a white hot spotlight being asked, "How many women have you been with before me?" suddenly it's not so fun anymore.

You guys know that at this point you usually don't actually start counting your sexual conquests. Instead, you begin to evaluate the woman you're with and try to figure out what answer would displease her the least. Too few, and she'll figure you're an inexperienced geek. Too many, you're a disloyal wolf. So rather than trying to come up with an honest answer, you're working to find that sexual experience "sweet spot" for this particular woman.

But guys, she's not really asking for a number! (See note at the bottom of the first question below.) Remember, as with all impossible questions, she's asking for reassurance. This is not only true regarding questions about sex but is *especially* true regarding questions about sex.

Now, you guys say a lot of things to your ladies that you don't even recognize as having to do with sex. Suffice it to say, telling her that, "Hey, if guys were intended to take care of birth control, they'd put it in beer," will not endear you to her. And, "But we kiss," is never justification for using her toothbrush!

On a more serious note, questions about sex touch on some very deeply held feelings for both men and women, and discussions about this topic can be very serious. It's important that, while you should offer reassurance, you should also be truthful and follow through on any commitments you make to your lady. Screwing up on these can end up being deal breakers.

Finally, a lot of questions about sex come disguised as questions about how she looks, which we've covered in Chapter 2. So hopefully, you've already learned something. Here's what you can do with these more obvious questions about sex.

Tip: Don't get graphic, offer reassurance!

How many women have you been with before me?*

Translation: I think you may be so experienced that I'm worried I'll pale by comparison.

Wrong answer: Who knows! I lost count a long time ago. Ha ha

She hears: You'll never live up to my memories of others.

Right answer: None of them made me feel as good as I do when I'm with you! (Or if you haven't been with her yet: I have a strong

feeling those memories will be totally wiped out once I've been with you!) *

She hears: You're the woman I remember best (or expect to remember best) and want to be with. (She's reassured.)

* Note: If it's clear she's asking this question in the context of seeking your sexual history for health reasons, the only responsible answer is the <u>truth</u> in the form of a solid number. It is also your responsibility to disclose if you currently have or have ever had any sexually transmitted disease.

What's the best sex you've ever had?

Translation: I want to be the best sex you've ever had and I'm wondering if I'm enough for you.

Wrong answer: Let me think... (Or any hesitation or any story of any sex that doesn't involve her!)

She hears: I remember them all in detail and frequently review them mentally.

Right answer: Absolutely no contest... you! You're the best I've ever had. (Hug her and hold her until *she* lets go!)

She hears: I'm happy with you. I'm not going anywhere. (She's reassured.)

(In bed) Where did you learn *that*?

Translation: I'm concerned that you've been with someone else who taught you that move.

Wrong answer: From my girlfriend before you and I got together. We used to do it all the time. (Or I read about it, or I saw it on a web site.)

She hears: You haven't been giving me what I want or need.

Right answer: You're so sexy that you give me all kinds of naughty thoughts and ideas for new things to try!

She hears: I'm thinking about you! (She's reassured.)

I didn't get around to shaving and don't really want to. Do you care?

Translation: Am I sexy to you even when I'm not at my very best?

Wrong answer: Go ahead and take a minute to do it. I think you'll feel better.

She hears: You disgust me as you are at this moment. Shave so I'll feel better.

Right answer: You're perfect exactly as you are right this minute! Come here! I don't want to wait another minute!

She hears: I love and want you even when you aren't at your most perfect. (She's reassured.)

(In bed) Are you *serious* about what you suggested we try?

Translation: I'm not quite sure I want to do that.

Wrong answer: Yep! Absolutely serious! It's something I really want to do.

She hears: I don't care what you want. It's all about what I want.

Right answer: I thought it might be fun. But if you feel uncomfortable, I don't mind if we just let go of it. What we do now is more than enough to keep me happy the rest of my life!

She hears: You and what you offer are plenty. (She's reassured.)

You say you like sexy lingerie. So why do you want it on the floor before we've barely started?

Translation: I feel sexy in this stuff and want to wear it a bit longer.

Wrong answer: It just gets in the way of that sexy body.

She hears: I lied. I don't really like sexy lingerie. I like naked!

Right answer: I look at you in it more than you realize. I sort of take a snapshot in my mind and look at it over and over while we're together. But let's try something new. Let's sort of "work around it" while you leave it on.

She hears: I do like seeing you in it and think about you in it. But I hear what you're saying and I want to please you. (She's reassured.)

I swear sometimes you treat me like a call girl in bed. Is that how you see me?

Translation: Sometimes I wonder if you really respect me.

Wrong answer: Geez! How can you say that? You always have to make every little thing into a big deal.

She hears: You're overreacting and immature.

Right answer: Come on now. I thought we were just having fun. You know I cherish you and think the absolute world of you.

She hears: I respect you even if I do sometimes get carried away in bed. (She's reassured.)

I saw you checking her out. Do you wish I looked like that?

Translation: I'm afraid I'm not attractive enough to hold your attention.

Wrong answer: She's got cute _____. (Naming any part of her anatomy whether considered sexual or not).

She hears: You've lost my attention and I'll be checking out other women from now on.

Right answer: Her? She can't hold a candle to you! She's not nearly as gorgeous as you are.

She hears: You're much prettier and you still have my attention. (She's reassured.)

(In bed) Did you just call me by your ex's name?

Translation: I'm worried that you're thinking about your ex while you're in bed with me.

Wrong answer: No. You're nuts. I didn't just call you anything.

She hears: You caught me but I'm going to try to lie my way out of this one.

Right answer: Did I? I'm sorry. But I promise I know who I'm with and I'm thinking only of you!

She hears: I am fully present here and I am thinking only of you. (She's reassured.)

Why do you look at that stuff on-line? Aren't I enough for you?

Translation: I feel very insecure when you do that and it makes me feel unsure of my ability to hold your attention.

Wrong answer: It's not like it's real. They're just strangers I'll never meet!

She hears: I need to look at this stuff to fill the huge gap you leave in satisfying me.

Right answer: You're absolutely enough for me! Guys are wired differently. We can be completely in love with a woman who satisfies us fully and still look at this stuff just for entertainment. But if it bothers you, let's talk about it.

She hears: I love only you and looking at this stuff says nothing about my feelings for you or our relationship. I'm willing to discuss it. (She's reassured.)

The bottom line on questions about sex: If a woman asks you any impossible question that has anything at all to do with sex, she's asking for reassurance. She wants to hear that you respect her, that you think she's sexy, that she alone meets your needs, and that your focus is on her. She also wants to be reassured that as the relationship continues you'll still find her attractive, will want her physically, and that you'll remain faithful.

Chapter 10

<u>Those Dreaded Hypotheticals</u>

In the wonderful Kevin Costner movie "For the Love of the Game", the leading lady, Kelly Preston, asks Costner, "Would you still love me if I got burned in a fire?"

He says, "Yes."

"If I ran into a tree and got paralyzed?"

He says, "Yes."

"What if I were totally disfigured, if my face was totally scraped away, I had no arms, no legs, no brain waves, and I was being kept alive on a heart-lung machine, would you still love me?"

He says, "No. But we could be friends."

Ah, that special brand of question that really frustrate logic-minded guys; hypothetical questions. Like it isn't tough enough answering all those impossible questions about the real world, women have to branch out into a whole new category of quiz show by asking guys questions about what might happen "if..."

If you're old enough to have learned how to read this, then you've probably figured out by now that women are much fonder of talking about feelings than guys are. And they love to hear about *your* feelings, particularly your feelings for *them*.

But sometimes you're just not in the mood to tell her how you feel and you begin to answer all her questions with a grunt. So often these impossible hypothetical questions are just a way for women to hear what they're longing to hear.

While women ask...

"What if I was really, really short?"
"What if I was kind of dumb?"
"What if I had a really high, squeaky voice?"

Guys think...

"What if there was no such thing as a hypothetical question?"

"If"... that's the word to look for. Almost without exception, the word "if" plays a critical role in hypothetical questions. "What would you do if...", "What would you say if...", "If I died would you...", and so on. Hey, after a whole slew of these, that last question doesn't sound so bad, right?

Tip: Don't be evasive, offer reassurance!

Would you still love me if I weighed 300 pounds?

Translation: Is it *me* you love or my body?

Wrong answer: Heck, I don't know. You'd never let yourself get that big.

She hears: No, I wouldn't love you if you were that fat.

Right answer: Yes! And I'd love you even if you were a cat! I'd love you if you were a giraffe! If you were a dragonfly, I'd figure out how to become a dragonfly too so I could be with you!

She hears: I love you no matter what form you take. (She's reassured.)

What will we do if one of us loses our job?

Translation: I'm worried about our financial future.

Wrong answer: Why? Are you about to get fired?

She hears: I always knew you were going to screw up at work.

Right answer: I don't think that'll happen. But if it does, we'll be okay. We have savings and we have skills. And best of all, we have each other!

She hears: No matter what, we'll be okay and I'm with you. (She's reassured.)

What if I get really sick?

Translation: I'm feeling scared and alone in the world right now and need to hear that you're there for me.

Wrong answer: Why do you always have to go looking for trouble? You're fine.

She hears: Yes, you're alone in the world and if you get sick I'm out of here.

Right answer: I don't think that'll happen. We're getting better about taking care of ourselves. And if you do get sick, I'll be here for you in a big way! (Give her a long hug!)

She hears: Your fears about becoming ill aren't going to come true. And, God forbid, if they do, I'll be here until the bitter end. (She's reassured.)

If someone falls on our steps outside we could be sued. What if that happens?

Translation: I'm scared about our liability and the financial hardships it could cause us.

Wrong answer: (Sarcastically) Well, how about we just not own anything at all and then we won't have to worry about such things. How about that?

She hears: I think your fears are absurd.

Right answer: I understand your concern. I think it's very unlikely to happen. But if it does, we have really good insurance to protect us.

She hears: I'm taking your concerns seriously and we'll be fine even if your fears come true. (She's reassured.)

What if your mother doesn't like her birthday gift?

Translation: I know you want to please your mother but I really want to just please you.

Wrong answer: Why on earth did you pick it out if you weren't sure she'd like it?

She hears: If she doesn't like it, then it's your fault and I'll be angry with you.

Right answer: I know you put a lot of thought and effort into selecting and wrapping her gift and I appreciate that so much. Please don't worry about it. Whether she likes it or not, *I* know you did a great job.

She hears: I know you worked hard and I appreciate that, whether my mother does or not. (She's reassured.)

What if it doesn't snow for our ski trip?

Translation: I want our vacation to be perfect and I'm worried about things I can't control.

Wrong answer: What the heck do you expect me to do about that?

She hears: If I can't control it, I don't want to hear about it.

Right answer: I'm sure it will. Besides, even if it doesn't snow, there are a lot of really fun things to do at the resort. We'll have a great time either way!

She hears: Don't worry. The success of our vacation doesn't pivot on things you can't control. (She's reassured.)

What will I do if I forget my speech?

Translation: I'm scared of making a fool of myself.

Wrong answer: Don't worry. Nobody ever actually listens to speeches anyway.

She hears: All your efforts are for nothing.

Right answer: You've read it, memorized it, and practiced it. You've rehearsed in front of the mirror and in front of me. There's absolutely no way on earth you'll forget your speech. Relax. You're going to do great!

She hears: I believe in you and you'll do great! (She's reassured.)

What if those pictures end up on Facebook?

Translation: I'm scared I'll be embarrassed or even mortified by a public display of photos taken of me.

Wrong answer: Don't worry. Nobody would post those on Facebook for free when they could blackmail you with them instead. Ha ha

She hears: The things that worry you are so trivial I consider them a joke.

Right answer: I know you're worried. But you didn't do anything to be ashamed of and I doubt they'll even get posted. Even if they do, hardly anyone will see them. So really, you don't have anything to worry about.

She hears: I understand how you feel but everything's going to be okay. (She's reassured.)

How will we stay together if we end up at different colleges?

Translation: I'm worried we're going to break up if we're living in different cities.

Wrong answer: Either we will or we won't.

She hears: I'm not worried about this because I just don't care.

Right answer: Hey, there's no reason to worry about that because we'll never let anything come between us—even if the miles do.

She hears: We are not going to break up even if we're far away from each other. (She's reassured.)

What if our baby is born with disabilities?

Translation: I'm scared about the health of our unborn child and about our ability to handle challenges that may be on the way.

Wrong answer: Geez... here we go again. Can't you just be happy without thinking the world is about to end?

She hears: You're an alarmist and therefore you're right. You aren't ready to handle the challenges of motherhood.

Right answer: The doctor says everything looks just fine. There's no reason at all to expect anything other than a healthy baby. And if the extremely unlikely happens, we handle it together.

She hears: We're going to have a healthy baby and if we don't, we'll still do just fine. (She's reassured.)

The bottom line on hypothetical questions: If a woman asks you any impossible question that is just a big "if" question (a hypothetical)—she's not trying to get you to cross some distant, imaginary bridge. She's seeking reassurance. She's asking for your reassurance that even if her worst fears come true, things are going to turn out okay and you'll be there for her. Reassure her that you love her no matter what and that, together, you guys are capable of handling whatever the world throws at you.

Chapter 11

<u>Argumentative Questions</u>

As you've learned in all the chapters above, impossible questions that women ask are not really questions at all. And no category of question could be more of a non-question than argumentative questions.

Just as in the courtroom, a woman's argumentative questions don't seek to establish additional facts or check the reliability of existing facts. Instead, they're meant only to "cause the witness to argue with the examiner". In other words, they're looking for a fight!

Think of these questions as "escalators" because they'll definitely escalate a guy's emotions. These are questions like, "What is *wrong* with you?" and "When will you *ever* learn?" Most guys, when they hear these kinds of questions, immediately feel compelled to either get physical or walk out. They call this stress reaction the "fight or flight" response.

When it comes to argumentative questions, a lot of guys want to prove that they're right. But the closest you'll get to a concession from a woman at this point is that she may say, "Well I'll admit you're wrong, if you'll admit I'm right!"

When you find yourself digging in your heels, there are two questions you should ask yourself which will help tremendously. The first is, "Do I want to be right or do I want to be happy?" Often you can't have both. So this will remind yourself that there may be a better goal than proving your point. Try to focus on resolving the disagreement instead. The second question to ask yourself is, "Is this something I'm fighting *for* or is this something I'm merely fighting *about*?" It's amazing how often we will argue over things that just aren't that important.

Believe me, the secret to winning an argument with a woman is still very much a secret. Do yourself a favor—agree with her. She's going to win anyway so you might as well be on the winning side.

So, as tempted as you are, the next time your lady hits you with one of these impossible questions, rather than slam your fist on the table and shout, "Objection! Argumentative!" I suggest you try answering with "The Right Answer™" instead.

Tip: Don't get angry, offer reassurance!

What is *wrong* with you?

Translation: I'm very frustrated with the way you're behaving.

Wrong answer: What's wrong is that I'm with you. That's what's wrong!

She hears: My behavior is just fine. It's your expectations that are wrong.

Right answer: (Calmly) You know, it really hurts when you speak to me that way. I get that you're mad. But can we talk about this without throwing barbs at each other?

She hears: You're words wound me but I'm willing to talk calmly. (She's reassured.)

When will you *ever* learn?

Translation: I keep telling you what I need and you never respond.

Wrong answer: Obviously I haven't learned yet or I wouldn't still be with you!

She hears: When I finally learn, I'm leaving you.

Right answer: Just because I don't agree, doesn't mean I don't understand. So please don't insinuate that I'm dense. It's insulting.

She hears: I understand what you want. Please don't imply I'm stupid. (She's reassured.)

How many times do I have to tell you?

Translation: It feels like you don't care enough to listen.

Wrong answer: I don't know. It's so much fun why don't you tell me again and we'll see if that finally does it!

She hears: Say it again so I can ignore you again.

Right answer: I admit it. I missed it. But I'm listening now. (Look her in the eye and listen!)

She hears: I care what you have to say to me. (She's reassured.)

Why won't you ever talk about this?

Translation: You're avoiding discussing this subject and I know it.

Wrong answer: Because we've beat this subject like a dead horse. Give it a rest already!

She hears: You talk and talk and I never listen so quit wasting your breath.

Right answer: Because it seems like there's nothing new to say about this. But I know you wouldn't keep talking about it if you felt you'd been heard. Listen, I don't want to argue so I'm willing to listen again.

She hears: I'm not getting what you're saying but I want to understand, so I'll listen. (She's reassured.)

How come you *always* do just what you want?

Translation: I feel like you don't consider my wants and needs.

Wrong answer: Trust me, if I was doing just what I wanted, it would be a lot different than what I'm doing now!

She hears: I actually want to behave much worse and I'm only reining it in this much to shut you up.

Right answer: Be fair. I don't *always* do what I want. I consider your feelings in all my decisions. But it won't always be 100% what you'd like because I'm a thinking adult and not a child.

She hears: I consider your feelings in my decisions but we may not always agree. (She's reassured.)

Why can't you just be supportive for a change?

Translation: I want you to agree with me whether we see eye to eye or not.

Wrong answer: I'm not going to support you when you're being crazy!

She hears: You're nuts and I'm reasonable and therefore I'm in charge.

Right answer: You know I'm always supportive of you when you're making good choices. But disagreeing with you when I think you're making a decision you'll regret is a form of support as well.

She hears: I care about you and I'm just giving my thoughts on this. (She's reassured.)

How come you always have to be so hurtful?

Translation: You've hurt me.

Wrong answer: How come you always have to be such a nag?

She hears: I hurt you in retaliation for being a thorn in my side.

Right answer: You know I'd never hurt you on purpose. And if I have this time, then I'm sorry. I guess I lose my temper when I feel like you go over things again and again.

She hears: I don't want to hurt you. I'm sorry. Please don't nag. (She's reassured.)

Why don't you ever care about the things that matter to me?

Translation: I want you to be interested in the things that are important to me.

Wrong answer: Some day you'll figure out that I will never be enthusiastic about (opera, French, reading, or whatever).

She hears: I don't love (opera, French, reading, or whatever) and so I don't love you.

Right answer: I'm glad you have things that matter to you. But I know you don't care about (NASCAR, computers, fishing, or whatever) and I understand it doesn't say anything about how you feel about me. I love you even if I don't love everything *you* love!

She hears: I can love you without loving (French, reading, or whatever). (She's reassured.)

Why do you always say I'm overreacting?

Translation: You treat me like I'm a hysterical woman.

Wrong answer: Because you *are* overreacting!

She hears: You *are* a hysterical woman.

Right answer: It does feel like you get upset and then can't even really hear what I'm trying to say. Can we both take a deep breath and listen to each other?

She hears: I want us to listen to and understand each other. (She's reassured.)

If you don't know, why should I tell you?

Translation: You can't seem to see the obvious, which really frustrates me.

Wrong answer: Fine! Don't tell me. It just saves me all the grief anyway.

She hears: I don't see it because I don't want to. I don't want to discuss it with you anyway.

Right answer: I really want to get better at understanding. But that's not going to happen if you won't tell me what you're really thinking.

She hears: I care about what is upsetting you and want to hear what you have to say. (She's reassured.)

The bottom line on argumentative questions: If a woman asks you any question that's truly argumentative, remember that it's not a question at all. She's most likely crossed the line into true anger. Don't join her. Don't get angry. Reassure her that you love her, you're willing to listen to and think about what's troubling her, and that together you guys are capable of calmly working out a solution.

Chapter 12

The Most Dangerous Questions

"Dear," asks the wife, "would you remarry if I died?"

Searching his mind for the right answer he says, "No, of course not, Honey."

"Don't you like being married?" asks the wife dejectedly.

"Of course I do, Honey," he says. Then, performing an about-face, "Now that I think about it, I'd definitely remarry."

"You would?" asks the wife as she looks vaguely hurt.

"Yeah... uh... sure," says the husband, not wanting to change his position yet again.

"Would you take down the pictures of me and put up hers?" she asks.

"I guess I'd have to," the husband says.

"Would you sleep with her in our bed and let her wear my clothes?" asks the wife.

"Well yes, I suppose I would," replies the husband.

"I see," says the wife indignantly. "And would you even let her use my golf clubs?"

"Of course not, dear," says the husband. "She's left-handed."

While all the questions in this book are dangerous questions, I've saved the best for last. These are the ones that even the most clueless guy recognizes as treacherous territory. These are the questions that if repeated to his 'bros' in the locker room, will result in the same facial expressions and sympathetic groans as if he related a story about being hit with a baseball in the privates (without a cup). You've all had them, you all hate them, and you're all still trying to figure out the right answer.

Now, I'd be remiss if I didn't warn you that often, timing is every bit as important as the answer when it comes to dangerous questions. Answering too quickly or too slowly can actually get you in as much hot water as the answer itself. For example, "Which of my friends do you think is the prettiest?" or "Do you think we should live near my mother?" if answered too quickly indicates you've given the subject prior consideration—never a good idea. And any delay at all in answering, "Have you ever considered leaving me?" or "Do you like my new hairstyle?" will buy you a slew of follow-ups which will *not* be a pleasant experience.

So keep in mind that the moment a woman asks one of these dangerous questions, the wrong answer will cause her to instantly begin to channel Glenn Close in Fatal Attraction (and not the sweet, early-in-the-movie character but the crazed, end-of-the-movie one). So read the examples below and study them. And I suggest you get the idea here guys, or prepare to have your bunny boiled.

Tip: Don't panic, offer reassurance!

Who would you marry if I died?

> Translation: I need to hear you'd miss me if I was gone.

> Wrong answer: (The name of any woman anywhere.)

She hears: I often fantasize about (the name you mentioned).

Right answer: Marry? Are you kidding? I'd crawl into your coffin and be buried with you because my life would be over if you died!

She hears: I can't imagine life without you. (She's reassured.)

Do you consider me high maintenance?

Translation: I really hope you think I'm worth your trouble.

Wrong answer: Yeah. You're a diva if I ever met one.

She hears: You're a pain in the butt and I sometimes wonder why I keep you around.

Right answer: High Maintenance? No way! You're no trouble at all. Listen, when it comes to us as a couple I know I came out way ahead in this deal.

She hears: I'm thrilled to be with you and have no regrets. (She's reassured.)

Do you think she's pretty (sexy, hot, etc.)?

Translation: I hope you think *I'm* pretty (sexy, hot, etc.).

Wrong answer: Sure, she's pretty.

She hears: I'm constantly evaluating other women as options and she's high up on the list.

Right answer: Her? You've got to be kidding. She's nowhere near as pretty as you!

She hears: You are the best looking woman I know. (She's reassured.)

Where do you see this relationship going?

Translation: I want our relationship to get more serious.

Wrong answer: Geez! Do we really have to talk about the relationship again?

She hears: You're annoying me and therefore chipping away at any hope of this relationship getting deeper or improving in any way.

Right answer: What we've got going is very important to me. I'll do whatever I need to do to be sure we have a solid, growing relationship that keeps getting better and better.

She hears: Our relationship matters to me and I want to nurture it and see it grow. (She's reassured.)

You're so quiet. What are you thinking about?

Translation: I feel shut out and want to know what you're feeling.

Wrong answer: Why do you always assume I'm thinking something?

She hears: I'm not going to let you in and certainly won't tell you my most private thoughts.

Right answer: Have I been quiet? My mind's just wandering. When I'm like this it's not even "thinking". Guys can be pretty shallow sometimes. I'm remembering sports, computer games, like that...

She hears: I'm not hiding anything from you. (She's reassured.)

If you had to change one thing about me, what would it be?

Translation: I want to know what you like least about me.

Wrong answer: I'd make you someone who doesn't ask so many questions!

She hears: I don't like talking to you.

Right answer: I'd go back in time and find you sooner and make you fall in love with me quicker!

She hears: You are so perfect that I only wish I found you sooner. (She's reassured.)

Would you care if someday my mother moved in with us?

Translation: I want to hear you love me enough to suffer for me.

Wrong answer: Are you kidding me? No way! She moves in, I move out!

She hears: I won't even pretend to love you enough to fake the right answer on this one.

Right answer: Well that's a long time off, if ever. I know you want your mother safe and happy. When the time comes, we'll make sure she is well taken care of.

She hears: I'm not willing to consent to your mom moving in. But I am going to let you know I care about you and about your concerns for your mom's future. (She's reassured.)

Who do you think is smarter—you or me?

Translation: I wonder if you really think you're smarter than me.

Wrong answer: Come on now. I'm not going there.

She hears: Of course I think I'm smarter than you but I refuse to upset you by saying so outright.

Right answer: I'll tell you a secret. We men often suspect that you women are smarter than we are. We may know how to fix things, but you women know how to get us to do it!

She hears: I respect your intelligence. (She's reassured.)

Don't you think we could benefit from seeing a therapist?

Translation: I think our relationship needs help.

Wrong answer: Do you really want me to answer that?

She hears: I think our relationship is a lost cause.

Right answer: I know we're working through some things right now. But I'm willing to talk about what we can do to make it better.

She hears: I'm aware of the issues and I want to work on it. (She's reassured.)

And finally, in the ultimate irony, the final question is...

Do I ask you too many questions?

Translation: I need to know if you hate these talks I force you to have.

Wrong answer: Heck yeah!

She hears: I'd never talk to you again if I could get away with it.

Right answer: I know you ask because you want to know me better and I'm flattered. But the truth is, sometimes I don't feel like answering questions.

She hears: I love talking with you, but sometimes I need my solitude. (She's reassured.)

The bottom line on the most dangerous questions: If a woman asks you any question that falls into the category of dangerous, remember, don't panic. You very well may not have to answer the question at all. Stop, translate, and figure out what she needs reassurance about and then offer it. But don't forget, the timing of your answer may be as important as the answer itself.

Chapter 13

<u>The Exception to the Rule</u>

Sigmund Freud was a psychologist who was well known for dream interpretation. He believed that every object in our dreams actually represents a deeper, more personally significant meaning. From what I can tell, he also seemed to believe nearly everything signified repressed thinking about sex. For example, water might represent thirst—a thirst for sex. And melons might represent breasts and a desire for sex. And the moon might represent a big round... well you get where he was going with all this. But he also said, "Sometimes a cigar is just a cigar."

So just when you're getting good at this, I'm going to throw you a couple of curve balls (pardon the reference there, guys). You've got to recognize that not *every* question a woman asks is an impossible question that needs to be "translated". Obviously, women aren't *always* seeking reassurance. Occasionally, a woman's question is just seeking information or making a request. These are simple questions with simple answers.

An attempt to reassure in the wrong instance can be counterproductive and will only aggravate the woman. Imagine your lady is late for work, is frantically looking around, and asks you if you've seen her keys. If rather than hopping up and beginning to lift couch pillows, you sat reading your paper and answered with a reassuring, "Honey, I understand you're feeling concerned about making it to work on time. But I have all the confidence in the world in your searching abilities. I'm sure you'll find the keys I saw Junior playing with earlier today." I can pretty much guarantee that not only will you and your lady not sleep together that night, but you may be looking for your own keys wearing scuba gear.

Here's how you can tell the two kinds of questions apart:

<u>Simple questions with simple answers:</u> Often, but not always, simple questions can be answered with yes or no or other simple facts. Generally she'll be busy and moving about when she asks these kinds of simple questions. If you hear a clear request, it's often just a simple question. If the word "please" is in the sentence it's also most likely a simple request or question. If you don't really get that gut-check "uh oh" feeling when she asks, it *may* just be a simple question.

<u>Impossible questions that require translating and the right answer:</u> Generally, impossible questions occur when a woman is in a contemplative mood. She may be wistful and usually will ask impossible questions at a time when she's feeling sad, vulnerable, or second-guessing herself. Usually these take place while the two of you are driving in the car, lying in bed, on the phone, or in other relatively private moments. If you hear a question and suddenly get the feeling you're in the middle of a minefield, chances are it's an impossible question...

Stop... Translate... Reassure!

This book is filled with examples of impossible questions. Below is a list of simple questions. Read through them, you'll sense the difference.

What time will you be home today?

Did you remember to turn off the coffee maker?

How much do you think the property taxes will be this year?

Can you please pick up the dry cleaning today?

Are we out of light bulbs again?

Did you get those invitations mailed last week?

Are you available to drive the kids to practice?

Where'd you put the remote?

Do you want spaghetti or tacos tonight?

Where do you think I might have left the tool box?

Did you call your mom to wish her happy birthday?

What time is that show that we wanted to watch tonight?

Did the kids leave their bikes in the driveway again?

Will you please try to find time to mow the lawn this weekend?

Have you seen my phone?

Bonus Chapter

<u>What Never, Ever to Say!</u>

There are a lot of things guys say that never go over well. You guys generally recognize these things after the fact by the tears, slammed doors, and lack of sex. But by then it's too late. So I'm giving you this bonus chapter to tell you, in advance, what you should never, ever, say to a woman.

I could go into detail about why these are horrible, terrible, ugly things to say, but it just doesn't matter. Memorize this list and never, ever say any of them if you want to avoid the dog house. You can't say you weren't warned!

I wish I'd had a chance to see you in your prime.

Have you gained a few pounds?

Maybe my mom could show you how she does it.

If you can't handle the truth, don't ask the question!

Do you ever shut up?

That (fill in any name here) sure can cook!

I was counting on your intuition to know that I was lying.

Do we have to actually talk?

When's your birthday (our anniversary) again?

Why do you go so crazy all the time?

You're in the top two best looking women I've ever been with.

Stop nagging me!

Are you going to wear *that*?

Don't tell me unless I'm about to forget.

Don't worry. I've gotten used to it (or you).

Women your age... (followed by anything at all).

It must be your time of the month.

Were you even listening when I said...?

If it was easy I would have done it already.

At least I don't beat you!

Yeah, well, that was before you had kids.

Why do you have to have so many shoes (purses, books, etc.)?

Did you mean for your hair to look like that?

Maybe you're just not the mothering type.

You'll never amount to anything.

I just knew you'd go ballistic!

You look so good I didn't even recognize you.

I hate it when you do that!

We met because my buddy said you were a sure thing.

Did you make that dress yourself or what?

I saw this commercial for... (any beauty/weight loss product).

Why do you always do that? (No matter what "that" is).

You took that long to look like *this*?

I'd explain it but you wouldn't understand.

Have you ever considered a boob job?

There's medicine for that now (no matter what "that" is).

Why do you take so long to get ready?

You're smart to do your laundry on Saturday night while all your friends are out anyway.

So the diet isn't working, huh?

That outfit is great. It really hides all your figure flaws.

No offense, but... (followed by anything).

Your standards are too high.

Why are you always so touchy?

You're aging well.

That haircut really slims your face.

You're a... (any derogatory word for a woman—and you know what they are!)

You could never make it without me.

Women are irrational.

You clean up nicely.

Have you considered joining a gym?

You bring out the worst in me.

Are those stripper boots or what?

You drive very well for a woman.

Here, just let me do it! (Said in a frustrated way.)

She's so smokin' hot!

My ex used to do it this way (or never used to, etc.)

You look great for your age.

You're so pretty I don't even notice the extra weight.

I lied because I didn't want to hurt you.

You don't sweat much for a girl.

You look like you're sick or something.

You'd be a knock out if only... (any suggestion at all).

I figured it was better to ask forgiveness than to seek permission. (Men think it's so clever but women hate this stupid saying!)

I earn the money; I'll decide how to spend it.

Should you be eating that?

What did you do all day?

Pick yourself out something—we'll say it's from me.

I don't mean to be critical but... (followed by anything).

You're just not the marrying kind.

You're just like your mother!

(And finally with a nod to Jack Nicholson in "Something's Gotta Give"...)

I've always told you some version of the truth.

Bonus, Bonus Chapter

<u>You Can Never Go Wrong With...</u>

It occurred to me that I just spent an entire chapter telling you what never, ever to say. So I've decided to give you a bonus, bonus chapter. These are things you can say to your lady anytime, anywhere, which will always be well received. In fact, by sprinkling these in among all the times you give "The Right Answer™", you'll be accelerating the effect of those answers.

But remember, the road to success is always under construction. You may say the wrong thing now and again. Just keep thinking about what you've learned here.

And now, as I close, I wish you much success with your lady!

Can I get you anything (your pet name for her here)?

You're the best thing that ever happened to me!

I don't know what I'd do without you.

You're so beautiful!

My life would be empty without you.

I'm so glad you're mine.

I want to make you the happiest woman in the world.

How's your day going so far?

My fun times would not be nearly as fun without you.

Thanks for everything you do for me and our family.

Wow! You look great!

How'd I get so lucky as to be the guy who got you?

I'm so glad you love me.

You absolutely brighten my day, you know that?

You're my girl!

Just you and me, just you and me!

When we married, I got the better end of the deal, you know.

I just love looking at you, you know that?

You make me very happy!

You're truly a remarkable person.

I'm the luckiest man in the world because you love me.

You have an amazing soul.

And never forget the tried and true...

I love you!

The Right Answer™ To... Do I Look Fat In This?

And Other Impossible Questions Women Ask

Back of the Book Cheat Sheet

Impossible questions about...

<u>How she looks:</u> Don't give commentary. Reassure her that she looks absolutely terrific to you and that you're proud to be seen with her!

<u>The future:</u> Don't make predictions. Reassure her that she's capable, that you guys are strong as a couple and will face things together, and that her future is bright!

<u>The past:</u> Don't try to remember. Reassure her that you've both made good decisions and that she means the world to you even if you can't remember every last detail of the past.

<u>Her friends and family:</u> Don't furnish advice. Reassure her that you understand how important her friends and family are to her and that she has the ability to manage her important relationships skillfully.

<u>Your buddies and your family:</u> Don't get defensive. Reassure her that she is the most important person in your life and that no one has the power to negatively impact your opinion of her or your feelings for her.

<u>The house and kids:</u> Don't shirk responsibility. Reassure her that she has been and will be a great mom and that you will pitch in fairly with the house and kids.

<u>Money and jobs:</u> Don't be a know-it-all. Reassure her that past, present, and future finances are being well handled and that you are in control of your work and that her work is worthwhile.

<u>Sex:</u> Don't get graphic. Reassure her that you think she's sexy, you want her, you are faithful, and that this won't change.

<u>Hypothetical Questions:</u> Don't get frustrated. Reassure her that even if her worst fears come true, the two of you are capable of handling anything and that things are going to turn out just fine.

<u>Argumentative Questions:</u> Don't get angry. Reassure her that you want to understand what's making her angry and that you want to work with her to improve the situation.

<u>The Most Dangerous Questions:</u> Don't panic. Reassure her about what the question points towards. Remember to stop, translate, and reassure. But don't forget, the timing of your answer may be as important as the answer itself.

<u>Exception to the rule (Simple questions):</u> If it's just a simple sentence asking for information, don't over think it. Just give a simple answer.

<u>Avoid those "never, ever" say sentences!</u>

<u>Sprinkle in a whole lot of those "You can never go wrong with..." sentences!</u>

About the Author

I'm a Texas lady. I grew up in Houston, went to school in Austin, and then raised my kids in Dallas. Now I live on my ranch in central Texas. It's the real deal with cattle, tractors, snakes, campfires, and wildlife. Out here, we gauge how remote a place is by how long it takes to drive to the nearest Super Wal-Mart. It's about 45 minutes for me—one way. Needless to say, I try not to forget to buy the coffee.

When I'm not mending barbed wire fences, fishing for dinner, or chasing around the wildlife with my camera, I'm visiting family and friends. I go to Dallas to see family and to meet with my book group, an amazing collection of unlikely female friends who have been getting together once a month for fifteen years now. We've "listened to" each others' children grow up and shared the good, the bad, and the ugly of the many relationships in our lives.

I go to Houston to see family and meet with my elementary school friends. More than thirty years after "graduating" from grade school, we still feel close and enjoy sharing memories of the Mayberry-like community where we grew up.

And I go to Austin to visit the friends I made while a student at the University of Texas. Three of my other favorite cities to visit are Nashville, Washington, D.C., and Denver, where my children attended college and where my best friend lives.

I've always loved to read, and later, to write. I particularly love collections of letters and personal essays. My favorites run the gamut; Mark Twain, Stephen Leacock, Erma Bombeck, Montaigne, Emerson, Dave Berry, Churchill, and a whole slew of other syndicated columnists, politicians, and humorists.

Since I was quite young, I've always received very positive remarks on my letters and email. Family and friends have told me how much they enjoy my tone and how they look forward to reading more. In more recent years, I've received the same sort of comments from strangers when I post my thoughts in forums on the web.

Inevitably, it would be suggested that I consider writing professionally, but I would immediately dismiss the idea because I never wanted to deal with publishers. But with the advent of eBooks that was no longer an issue and so I decided to work on an idea that I'd had knocking around in my head for quite a while.

It's always seemed to me that traditional relationship books go about things unrealistically. It's as if they expect you to read a book on how to swim and then throw you into treacherous seas and expect you to keep your head above water. People need very practical advice. They need to know what to say. They need "The Right Answer™".

At this point, you may be asking yourself what special training I have which allows me to give advice on relationships. I have absolutely no formal credentials to offer. I'm not a psychiatrist, psychologist, or a marriage counselor. While those experts have much success helping people relate, not every relationship requires that level of specialized care.

What I do have to offer is that, as a very young girl, I was part of a military family back when the military was a very male-dominated, macho place. As I grew up, my favorite TV shows were those which focused on men and brotherly love such as Bonanza, The Rifleman, Adam-12, and Emergency.

When my parents divorced, I chose to live with my father while my siblings stayed with my mother. I attended an all-girl high school but always had a boyfriend. For almost thirty years I've been married to a man who has offered the right answer to all of my impossible questions. I've raised a son who is a man who, as he puts it, "gets it" when it comes to women's impossible questions. Finally, for more than twenty years I worked in aviation, a strongly male-dominated field.

The bottom line is that I genuinely like men and I understand them. And I genuinely like women and certainly understand them. Basically I'm the world's most feminine tomboy. This puts me in the unique position to be a "translator".

I believe most men really want to please women and don't want to say things to upset them needlessly. But when talking to women, men listen and speak like men and the end result is a lot of miscommunication, hurt feelings, and slammed doors. I wrote "The Right Answer™", purely out of my expertise as a woman who is fond of men and as someone who wants to make men's lives easier while simultaneously giving women what they need.

www.therightanswerbooks.com

www.ingramcontent.com/pod-product-compliance
Lightning Source LLC
Chambersburg PA
CBHW050540280326
41933CB00011B/1663